The Gingerbread Man

Retold by Annette Smith

Illustrated by Rachel Tonkin

Gingerbread man created by Nathan Mitchell

Once upon a time,
there was a little old man
and a little old woman.

One day,
the little old woman
made a gingerbread man.

She gave him a head,
two arms, and two legs.
She gave him two eyes,
a nose,
and a mouth.

CURRANTS

3

The little old woman
put the gingerbread man
into the oven to bake.

Soon the little old man said,
"I can smell gingerbread baking.
I will see
if the gingerbread man
is ready to eat."

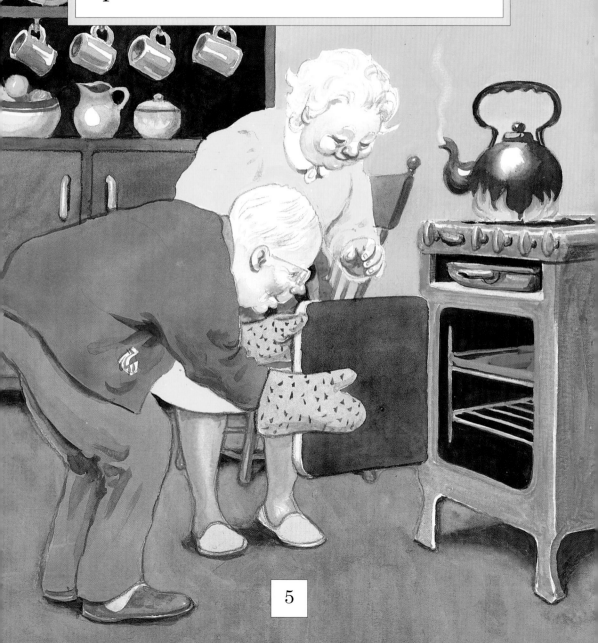

The little old man
opened the oven door.

Out jumped the gingerbread man.
He ran across the room
and out the door
as fast as he could go.

"Stop! Stop!"
called the little old man.

"Stop! Stop!"
called the little old woman.
"Come back!"

But the gingerbread man
laughed at them.
"Run, run,
as fast as you can.
You can't catch me,
I'm the gingerbread man."

7

The little old man and
the little old woman ran fast.
But the gingerbread man
ran faster.

The gingerbread man
ran on and on.
He met a cow.

"Stop! Stop!" called the cow.
"I want to eat you!"

The gingerbread man laughed
at the cow.
"*Run, run,*
as fast as you can.
You can't catch me,
I'm the gingerbread man."

The gingerbread man
ran on and on.
He met a horse.

"Stop! Stop!" called the horse.
"I want to eat you."

The gingerbread man laughed
at the horse.
"*Run, run,*
as fast as you can.
You can't catch me,
I'm the gingerbread man."

The gingerbread man
came to a river.
He stopped.
He could not get across.

A sly old fox
came up to him.
"I will take you across,"
the fox said.
"Climb onto my tail."

So the gingerbread man
climbed onto the fox's tail.

"Gingerbread man!"
called the fox.
"You are too heavy
for my tail.
Sit on my back."

So the gingerbread man
climbed onto the fox's back.

"Gingerbread man!"
called the fox.
"You are too heavy
for my back.
Sit on my nose."

But when the gingerbread
man sat on the fox's nose,
the fox
tossed him up
into the air.

Snip!

Snap!

The fox gobbled him up.

And that was the end
of the gingerbread man.

A play
The Gingerbread Man

People in the play

 Narrator

 Little Old Man

 Little Old Woman

 Gingerbread Man

 Cow

 Horse

 Sly Old Fox

Narrator

Once upon a time
there was a little old man
and a little old woman.
They lived all by themselves.

Little Old Woman

I'm going to make
a gingerbread man today.
This is his head.
Here are his arms,
and here are his legs.

Little Old Man

You can give him
two eyes and a nose
and a mouth as well.

Little Old Woman

Now the gingerbread man
is ready to be baked.
I will put him in the oven.

Narrator

The little old woman
put the gingerbread man
into the oven to bake.

Little Old Man

Mmm—mmm,
I can smell
the gingerbread baking.
I will see
if the gingerbread man
is ready to eat.

Narrator

The little old man
opened the oven door.
Out jumped the gingerbread man.

Little Old Man

Oh! Oh!
The gingerbread man
is going out the door.
He's running fast.
Stop! Stop!

Little Old Woman

Stop, gingerbread man!
Come back!

Gingerbread Man *(laughing)*

Run, run,
as fast as you can.
You can't catch me,
I'm the gingerbread man.

Little Old Man

Come on.
Let's go after him.

Little Old Woman

He's running too fast for us.
We can't catch him.

Narrator

The gingerbread man
ran on and on.
He met a cow.

Cow

Stop! Stop!
I want to eat you.

Gingerbread Man *(laughing)*

Run, run,
as fast as you can.
You can't catch me,
I'm the gingerbread man.

Cow

Stop! Come back here!

Gingerbread Man

I have run away
from a little old man
and a little old woman,
and I will run away
from you, too.

Narrator

The gingerbread man
ran on and on.
He met a horse.

Horse

Stop! Stop!
I want to eat you.

Gingerbread Man *(laughing)*

Run, run,
as fast as you can.
You can't catch me,
I'm the gingerbread man.

Horse

Stop! Come back here!

Narrator

Then the gingerbread man
came to a river.

Gingerbread Man

I can't get across this river.
The horse and the cow
and the little old woman
and the little old man
are coming.
They will catch me.
They want to eat me.

Narrator

A sly old fox came up
to the gingerbread man.

Sly Old Fox

Hello, gingerbread man.
I will take you over the river.
Climb onto my tail.

Gingerbread Man *(calling)*

I'm on your tail, fox.
You can swim over
the river, now.

Sly Old Fox

Gingerbread man,
gingerbread man,
you are too heavy for my tail.
Sit on my back.

Narrator

So the gingerbread man
climbed onto the fox's back.

Sly Old Fox

Gingerbread man,
gingerbread man,
you are too heavy for my back.
Sit on my nose.

Gingerbread Man

I can see
where we are going, now.
We will soon be
across the river.

Narrator

But the sly old fox
tossed the gingerbread man
up in the air.

Sly Old Fox

SNIP!   SNAP!

Narrator

And that was the end
of the gingerbread man.